LIFE'S LES

Words of Wisdom to Help You
Lead a Better Life

BY HOWARD WIGHT

Copyright 1992 by Howard Wight. All rights reserved. This book, or any parts thereof, may not be reproduced in any form without written permission from the publisher. For information, please contact Wight Financial Concepts Corp., 44 Montgomery Street, Suite 2266, San Francisco, CA 94104. Telephone (800) 486-SELL.

Library of Congress Catalog Card Number: 92-91102
ISBN 0-9633506-1-7

INTRODUCTION

A word . . . a thought . . . an idea . . . a new perspective can change a lifetime . . . perhaps yours.

Sometimes you have to hear something one hundred times before it sinks in . . . before it makes a difference.

The only way I can truly thank those whose words have made a difference in my life is by adding to the collection and sharing it with you. I hope that these words, these lessons, will have a positive impact on your life.

Howard Wight
November, 1992

DEDICATION

In addition to all the people whose words have formed the foundation for this book, I would like to thank my assistants, Debra Ackerman and Rebecca Wallo, for their patience and hard work.

ACKNOWLEDGMENTS

To my children, David and Jennifer, whom I love very much, and who have paid a very high price for whatever success I may have achieved.

Success is about making a difference . . . not just about making money.

❏ Some people make things happen. Some people watch things happen. Some people don't know anything is happening.

❏ When you stop doing, you start dying.

❏ There's nothing to it but to do it.

❏ There is no one right way. Almost any way works if you do it a lot.

A word, a thought, a new idea, a new perspective . . . can change a lifetime.

❏ You don't get anywhere by figuring out 50 reasons why something can't be done.

❏ Some people get ready and then do something. Some just keep on getting ready.

❏ Doing less often means doing more.

❏ Momentum can't be hoarded. Use it or lose it.

Your consistent thoughts and actions become your reality.

- ❏ Don't try to do it all. Not all of it matters anyhow. What is important to you? Do it.

- ❏ If you have 100 things to do, do one. Get started. Now you only have 99 things left to do.

- ❏ Yesterday is a cancelled check. Tomorrow is a promissory note. Today is cash in the bank.

What you think and do is up to you.

Choices repeated become habits.

❑ Thinking often takes as much time as doing.

❑ Hard work is just an accumulation of easy work combined with procrastination.

❑ For perfectionists, preparation often becomes procrastination.

❑ You must get on with your life. The option is not an option.

Maintain a positive attitude.

Every problem is an opportunity.

Expect success.

❏ Doing something is almost always less costly than doing nothing.

❏ If you are ultimately going to do something important that will make a real difference . . . do it now.

❏ Perfectionists procrastinate. Pragmatists profit.

Decisions are easy when you know what's important to you. What is important?

❑ Repetition is the mother of learning, skill, and mastery.

❑ The truly wise person learns from the experience of others, as well as from his or her own experience. You don't have time to learn only from your own experience.

❑ Take charge of your life now. Get off automatic pilot.

What's important now? Ask,

"What is the best use of

my time now?"

Do it now.

- ❏ Read one book per week . . . fifty books per year.

- ❏ Change is inevitable. Growth is optional.

- ❏ Continually strive to practice what you preach.

- ❏ Attitude is to life as location is to real estate.

Planning produces profits. Establish goals, priorities, and deadlines.

- ❏ How you perceive yourself will be reflected in how you perceive others.

- ❏ The best is yet to come.

- ❏ Anger is a negative emotion which undermines your ability to succeed. Forgive others and yourself.

- ❏ Expect success.

Focus is the key to effectiveness.

Do the right things right.

First things first.

❑ I still experience peaks and valleys . . . but the valleys are now where the peaks used to be.

❑ Pessimists ask why. Optimists ask why not.

❑ Your perception is your reality.

❑ No one can make you feel bad about yourself without your consent.

Know what you know.

Know what you don't know.

Know when to say no.

❏ Sad or glad . . . your choice.

❏ Would you rather be around someone who is pretending to be positive or someone who is sincerely negative?

❏ Anger is fear in disguise.

❏ Believing you can is the first step on the road to accomplishment.

Life is hard by the yard

but a cinch by the inch.

Doing something does something.

- Nothing will change until you do.

- What you achieve is based on what you believe.

- Caring and enthusiasm are contagious.

- Change your attitude. Change your life.

Do what you do best and

delegate the rest.

Do more by doing less.

Reward results.

- ❏ Those consumed by anger and hate destroy only themselves.

- ❏ What you believe works . . . works.

- ❏ Don't complain about things that you can't or won't change.

- ❏ Attitude + Action = Accomplishment.

He who believes . . . succeeds.

He who doubts . . . fails.

Sell yourself first.

❏ What is the worst thing that ever happened to you? Did you survive? Of course. Use that experience to overcome other obstacles.

❏ Accentuate the positive. Eliminate the negative.

❏ Feeling good starts with a smile.

❏ To hang on to the past is to die a little each day.

The price is not the problem. Paying the price is the solution to the problem.

❏ Accept the things you cannot change.
  Change the things you cannot accept.

❏ Smile. A positive attitude will surely
  follow.

❏ If you have time to complain, you probably
  don't have enough work to do.

❏ Practice produces profits.

Lighten up.

He who laughs . . . lasts.

Will it really matter in 10 years

(or 10 days)?

❑ Managers are people who do things right. Leaders are people who do the right things.

❑ Some people choose not to participate in recessions. Business is good even when it's bad for others. When it's good for others, it's great for them.

❑ Good supervision is the art of getting average people to do superior work.

The primary purpose

of communication

is to effect change.

Keep it simple and sincere.

❑ If most executives paid the same attention to their businesses that they pay to their personal situations, they would be fired.

❑ Everyone makes mistakes. Your business can absorb the little mistakes. The big mistakes can absorb your business.

❑ Most managers maintain the minutes of meetings but lose hours.

Caring, chemistry, trust and timing are essential to good relationships.

❏ The greatest management principle is to reward people . . . each according to his or her own needs.

❏ If they don't buy the concept, the details are irrelevant.

❏ You become known by the customers you keep.

*Successful people consistently
do what others can do but don't.*

❑ People who know how to do something generally work for those who know what to do and why.

❑ What you think and do is up to you.

❑ Take charge of your life by consciously changing your choices.

❑ If it is to be . . . it is up to me.

You have already done what it takes to be successful. Just do it more often.

❑ The worst thing about making a mistake is attempting to justify it.

❑ If you had it all to do over again, what changes would you make?

❑ Good habits separate the best from the rest.

❑ Not to decide is to decide.

Persist.

Failing is not failure unless you

fail to try again.

Learn from experience.

❑ Your life is ultimately a reflection of the choices you make . . . one by one . . . day by day.

❑ We first form habits, and then the habits form us.

❑ When in doubt, throw it out.

❑ That was then. This is now. You can change your life starting now by changing your choices.

Consciously commit to success and excellence, or unconsciously accept mediocrity.

- ❑ Choices today impact results tomorrow.

- ❑ You may be doing something right . . . but should you be doing it?

- ❑ Life is about the choices we make and the chances we take.

- ❑ If you keep doing what you are doing, you will keep getting what you are getting.

> *"That man is a success who has laughed often and loved much; who has filled his niche and loved his task; who leaves the world better than he found it; who looked for the best in others and gave the best he had."*
>
> Robert Louis Stevenson

❏ Habits are choices repeated often.

❏ Truly fortunate is the person whose vocation and avocation is the same.

❏ Life is too short to accept mediocrity from yourself or others.

❏ Change your choices and you will change your life.

"Wise men speak because they have something to say.
Fools speak because they have to say something."

Plato

❑ Wisdom means knowing what to do.
Ability means knowing how to do it.
Commitment means doing it.
Conviction means knowing why.

❑ Competence and compassion are compatible. People don't care how much you know . . . until they know how much you care.

❑ If you put more in, you'll get more out.

"What is originality?

Undetected plagiarism."

Dean William R. Inge

- ❏ The sooner you pay the price, the lower the price and the bigger the payoff.

- ❏ Uncertainty undermines.

- ❏ One thing at a time, one step at a time, one day at a time.

- ❏ Consistency separates the great from the mediocre.

"A man who provides not for his own and specially those of his own house has denied the faith and is worse than an infidel."

St. Paul

- ❑ Cowards never start; the weak die along the way; only the strong survive.

- ❑ Often the reason people give for not doing something is the very reason why they should be doing it in the first place.

- ❑ Knowledge without the ability to communicate it effectively is meaningless.

"It's what you learn after you know it all that counts."

John Wooden

❏ Tell them what you are going to tell them. Tell them. Then tell them what you told them. Then ask them what you told them.

❏ For most people, it's simple to be complex and complex to be simple.

❏ Question. Listen. Pause. Think. Respond.

> *"Upon the fields of friendly strife are sown the seeds that, upon other fields, on other days, will bear the fruit of victory."*

General Douglas MacArthur

- ❏ As a general rule, anything that has to be shouted or whispered probably isn't worth listening to.

- ❏ The best preparation is preparing to listen.

- ❏ Life's lessons are learned by living and listening.

> *"A mind is a terrible thing to make up."*
>
> Jay Leno

- ❏ What you say about others often says more about you than about them.

- ❏ When in doubt, tell the truth.

- ❏ Tell me and I will forget. Show me and I will remember. Involve me and I will understand.

- ❏ Sometimes the strongest statement you can make is silence.

"People are always blaming their circumstances for what they are. I don't believe in circumstances. The people who get on in this world are the people who get up and look for the circumstances they want, and if they can't find them, make them."

George Bernard Shaw

- ❑ Avoid big words. Keep it simple and sincere. Eschew polysyllabic obfuscation.

- ❑ If you want to make an impact . . . . . pause.

- ❑ There are almost always two sides to every story. Both typically have merit.

- ❑ Most people hear what they want to hear and disregard the rest.

> *"The mind is its own place,*
> *and in itself*
> *can make a heaven of hell,*
> *a hell of heaven."*

John Milton

❑ You do not have to agree with someone in order to learn from him.

❑ A lot of people say absolutely nothing . . . but they say it very well.

❑ Understanding a problem is the first step toward solving it.

❑ You don't have to be disagreeable in order to disagree.

"Our greatest glory is not in never failing, but in rising every time we fall."

Thomas Carlisle

- ❑ The primary result of most communication is miscommunication.

- ❑ Dream great dreams. Ask why not rather than why.

- ❑ The people that grow are not the ones with the best circumstances; it's the people with the biggest dreams.

- ❑ Not all of your dreams will come true, but that is no reason not to pursue them.

> *"Men are best convinced by reasons they themselves discover."*
>
> Ben Franklin

❏ Everything starts with an idea . . . then a dream.

❏ There is nothing of significance that you cannot accomplish, unless you choose not to strive for it.

❏ Dreams are the foundation of future realities.

> *"I don't believe in failure.*
> *It is not failure if you*
> *enjoy the process."*

Oprah Winfrey

- ❏ People dream dreams. You can help convert their dreams to reality.

- ❏ You won't change the future without changing the present.

- ❏ Every journey starts with a single step.

- ❏ What you have done says more about you than what you say.

"The toughest thing about success is that you've got to keep on being a success."

Irving Berlin

❏ Don't confuse hard work and efficiency with effectiveness. Efficiency means doing things right. Effectiveness means doing the right things right.

❏ Don't be afraid of opposition; a kite rises against the wind.

❏ Are you busy or effective? Effective people make time for the important things in life by reducing the trivial pursuits in their lives.

> *"The great end of life is not knowledge but action."*
>
> Thomas Henry Huxley

- ❏ It's not how long or how hard you work that counts; it's what you accomplish at the end of each day.

- ❏ Is what you are doing working? If not, why not?

- ❏ Just to stay even, you have to get better.

- ❏ You pretty much get what you expect in life. Expect the best.

> *"Man must realize his own unimportance before he can realize his importance."*
>
> Winston Churchill

❑ Don't look for excuses and you won't find them.

❑ The first part of believing is wanting to.

❑ Do you want to be one of the people on the peak or one of the people in the pack?

❑ Your comfort zone is where you are.

"The quality of a person's life is in direct proportion to their commitment to excellence, regardless of their chosen field of endeavor."

Vince Lombardi

❑ What you believe determines what you expect. What you expect determines what you get.

❑ There is an upside to everything. Sometimes it just takes a while to figure it out.

❑ Most people hope for much but expect little.

"If you have no critics, you likely have no successes."

Malcolm Forbes

- ❏ You can fail without being a failure.

- ❏ Failure never hurt anyone. Unwillingness to fail hurts everyone.

- ❏ Failure and problems are stepping stones on the road to success.

- ❏ You haven't failed unless you quit trying.

> *"The price of greatness is responsibility."*
>
> Winston Churchill

❏ There are few mistakes in life which can't be corrected.

❏ Mistakes are opportunities for learning and improvement.

❏ You learn more from your setbacks than from your successes.

❏ Failure is an outlook, not an outcome.

> *"The best way to give advice to your children is to find out what they want and then advise them to do it."*

Harry Truman

❏ Focus on doing your best and not on comparing yourself to others.

❏ Losers focus on the path. Winners focus on the purpose.

❏ Focus on first things first, and the rest will fall into place.

❏ Persist and persevere pleasantly.

> *"Success comes from listening.*
> *I've never learned anything from*
> *talking."*

Lou Holtz

❏ To the extent that you live in the past, you limit your ability to live effectively in the present.

❏ Focus on the positive, but keep an eye on reality.

❏ Most people don't know what they don't know.

❏ When it comes to giving, some people stop at nothing.

"The obscure we see eventually.
The completely apparent takes
longer."

Edward R. Murrow

❏ It is not required that one be perfect in order to help others.

❏ Life isn't about what you get . . . it's about what you give.

❏ Give others the best you've got.

❏ You can only repay those who helped you by helping others.

"Good humor makes all things tolerable."

Henry Ward Beecher

❏ Give real service . . . not lip service.

❏ The greatest gift you can give someone else is your own happiness.

❏ If you don't know where you are going, you might not know when you get there.

❏ Direction is more important than speed.

"A problem well stated is a problem half solved."

Charles Kettering

❏ A good plan implemented now beats the perfect plan someday.

❏ Are your goals really your goals . . . or are they someone else's goals for you?

❏ Goals are dreams with deadlines.

❏ What would be your goal if you knew you couldn't fail? That's what your goal should be.

"There is only one success – to spend your life in your own way."

Christopher Morley

- Whatever you need, you already have.

- We are lucky to be who we are. There but for the grace of God go I.

- Would you trade your tomorrows for your yesterdays? Would you rather be in any other business? Would you rather live in any other country?

- Would you trade your problems for those of others?

> *"Some of us will do our jobs well and some will not, but we will all be judged by only one thing – the result."*
>
> Vince Lombardi

- ❏ Solitude is a blessing. Loneliness is a curse.

- ❏ Would you rather be right or happy?

- ❏ Happiness is not having what you want but wanting what you have.

- ❏ Do what you love. Love what you do.

- ❏ The truth is not always popular.

"Nothing is often a good thing to do, and always a good thing to say."

Will Durant

❏ Only a fool learns from his own experiences. The wise learn from the experiences of others.

❏ Ignorance is never an asset. Knowledge misdirected can be a liability.

❏ Thinking you know something and knowing you know it project an entirely different attitude.

> *"He is most powerful who has power over himself."*
>
> Seneca

- The more you know, the less you have to say. You have to know a lot to say a little.

- Knowing what to do and why is more important than knowing how to do it.

- You learn by listening, not by talking.

- If you know a lot . . . keep most of it to yourself.

"If there is any one 'secret' of effectiveness, it is concentration. Effective executives do first things first, and they do one thing at a time."

Peter Drucker

❏ Knowledge alone is not power. The ability to communicate knowledge and to get people to act on it is power.

❏ The more you know . . . the less you have to prove it.

❏ Never lose the ability to laugh, and more importantly, never lose the ability to laugh at yourself.

"Most people are about as happy

as they make up their minds

to be."

Abraham Lincoln

- ❏ The difference between tax avoidance and tax evasion is twenty years.

- ❏ It's not how much you leave but how much is left that counts.

- ❏ Money is worth no more than it costs. People make it worth more.

- ❏ Just enough to get by is not enough to get ahead.

"Pressure is when you're not adequately prepared."

Lou Holtz

- ❏ People should not be paid more just for getting older.

- ❏ Establish a line of credit before you need it. If you need it, you can't get it.

- ❏ Prosperous people have a proclivity toward productivity rather than procrastination.

- ❏ Money buys time.

"We shall not cease from exploration,
and the end to all our exploring
will be to arrive where we started
and know the place for the first time."

T.S. Eliot

❏ Those who spend first and save what's left generally work for those who save first and spend what's left.

❏ Don't be afraid to take a big step. You can't cross a chasm in two small steps.

❏ What is obvious to some . . . is invisible to others.

"People who don't take risks generally make about two big mistakes a year. People who do take risks generally make about two big mistakes a year."

Peter Drucker

- ❏ You don't get a second chance to make a good first impression.

- ❏ Open up to opportunities. Say yes to opportunity and no to negativism.

- ❏ The early bird gets the worm. The moral of this story is that it is better to be an early bird than an early worm.

"*Excuses simply do not wash.*
They never have and they never will.
I don't care what the issue is.
By the time you finish with all of the
excuses, you are still confronted
with the problem."

Harry Edwards

- ❏ If you don't ask people to buy, there's a good chance they won't.

- ❏ Optimism overcomes obstacles and opens up opportunities.

- ❏ Pursue your purpose with passion.

- ❏ If you are not over your head, you are not swimming.

"Nothing in the world can take the place of persistence.
Talent will not; nothing is more common than unsuccessful men with talent.
Genius will not; unrewarded genius is almost a proverb.
Education will not; the world is full of educated derelicts.
Persistence and determination alone are omnipotent!"

Calvin Coolidge

- ❏ Logic tires . . . emotion inspires.

- ❏ To be truly great, you have to experience both the peaks and the valleys.

- ❏ In order to get the fruit of the tree, you sometimes have to go out on a limb.

- ❏ If you feel better about what you are doing, you will do more of it.

"A man has got to know his limitations."

Clint Eastwood

- ❏ Give it what you've got.

- ❏ Want power may be more important than willpower.

- ❏ By persuading others, we convince ourselves.

- ❏ Enthusiasm is the fuel of success.

> *"It's amazing what you can accomplish in life when you don't care who gets the credit."*
>
> Bob Woodruff
> Coca-Cola Founder

- ❑ As a general rule, people are giving it their best shot.

- ❑ People like people like themselves.

- ❑ There is no substitute for civility. Good manners go a long way.

- ❑ Trust is the foundation of all good relationships.

❏ The only way you can truly repay those who helped you is by helping others.

❏ When you pay attention to what people want, people will pay attention to you.

❏ There are two types of people: those who care and those who don't. Which are you?

❏ To be interesting, be interested.

❏ Most people take personally what they shouldn't, and don't take personally what they should.

❏ Do people really change or just become who they are?

❏ If you think others have no problems, it is only because you don't know them very well.

- ❏ Distance has nothing to do with the closeness of a relationship.

- ❏ Avoid problem people.

- ❏ Reputation is valuable, but character is priceless.

- ❏ It's hard to take seriously people who take themselves too seriously.

❏ When you're wondering what people are thinking about you, they're probably not. They have other things on their minds.

❏ Some people make bland appear colorful.

❏ Very bright people have an immediate response to almost everything. That's not very bright.

❏ Everybody is somebody.

❏ Friendship requires effort. You have to work at it.

❏ Some people have the ability to change people's lives; some by being there on an intimate basis; some just by passing through.

❏ Cramming works in school, but not on a farm. Most important things in life take time. You can't plant the seeds today and harvest the crop tomorrow.

❏ Finish what you start. Before you start . . . plan.

❏ Most people spend most of their lives doing the wrong things wrong. Planning helps you do the right things right . . . right now.

❏ Decisions are easy when you know what's important to you.

❏ Measure twice. Cut once. Plan before acting.

❏ Failing to plan often means having to do something over again. If you don't have time to plan, how will you have time to do it over?

❏ What is the best use of my time now?

❏ Planning is the cornerstone of success and time management.

❏ If you don't know where you are going, you will probably end up somewhere else.

❏ A goal without a deadline is a wish, not a commitment.

❏ Success is doing what you do best . . . and delegating the rest.

❑ Planning is the best investment you will ever make.

❑ The best time to plan is before you have to. If you wait until you have to plan you're reacting, not planning, and your options are already limited.

❑ Learning from experience takes too long, unless it is the experience of others.

❑ When you reach for the stars, you may not get them, but you won't come up with a handful of mud either.

❑ Do it your way . . . but do it often.

❑ How many hours do you work per week? Have you ever asked yourself why? What is it all for? What's important to you?

- ❑ Your life is what you make it.

- ❑ If you know why you want something . . . you will find the way.

- ❑ Work hard on simple things which make a difference.

- ❑ Wage war on procrastination.

- Wage war on time wasters.

- When you know what's important to you and do it, life becomes a lot simpler.

- The price of freedom is individual responsibility.

- Wouldn't it be nice if those who are concerned about their rights were similarly concerned about their responsibilities?

- ❑ Just because something is legal does not mean it is right. Do the right thing.

- ❑ Responsibility is the price you pay for success.

- ❑ If you wouldn't want to see it on TV or read about it in the paper, don't do it.

- ❑ People feel better about themselves when they act responsibly.

- ❑ Our greatest struggles are fought within the boundaries of our own minds.

- ❑ After all our changes, we are more or less the same.

- ❑ The only real security is that which you create for yourself.

- ❑ Character is revealed more by reactions than action.

❏ Your weak points are revealed by what you fall for; your strong points are shown by what you stand for.

❏ Your worth as an individual does not depend on what others think of you.

❏ We all need heroes in order to know how far we can go. Most limitations are self-imposed.

❑ Give yourself credit for the things you do well each day.

❑ You can fight back when others put you down, but you can't fight back when you put yourself down.

❑ Life is about becoming who you are.

❑ If you are not enjoying yourself, it's a virtual certainty no one else will.

❏ Don't rely on others to be the source of your happiness.

❏ Look within for the solution.

❏ What we like least about others is often a reflection of what we like least about ourselves.

❏ It is a strength to know your weaknesses.

❏ You become the best you can be when you become yourself. Most people spend a lot of time trying to become someone else.

❏ The only person stopping you from being successful is yourself.

❏ You've got to go with what you've got. You already have what you truly need.

❏ You can do better than you think.
You can do better if you think.
You can do better, don't you think?

❏ Don't wait until you're perfect before
getting on with your life.

❏ When you stop getting better, you cease
being good.

❏ If you are not working on yourself, you're not working.

❏ When you solve the problems of others, you often solve your own.

❏ There is no challenge greater than the one to improve yourself.

❏ Be the best of whatever you are. That's success.

❏ Whether we like it or not, we owe most of our success to luck. Working hard and smart greatly enhances the probability of being lucky.

❏ Happiness lies in both the doing and the accomplishment.

❏ Success defined in terms of helping and serving others gives one a sense of purpose in life . . . a mission.

❏ Your life is ultimately a reflection of the choices (decisions) that you make one by one, minute by minute, day by day.

❏ The difference between success and mediocrity is commitment.

❏ For you to succeed, others need not fail.

❏ The longest journey starts with the first step. The hardest step is the first step.

- ❏ The road to success is always under repair.

- ❏ Success is a process, not an event.

- ❏ The only place success comes before work is in the dictionary.

- ❏ No rule for success will work if you don't.

- ❏ Success is one step on a journey called life . . . and once taken, it must be repeated.

- Focus + Attitude + Action + Commitment = Success.

- Success does not consist in never making mistakes, but in never making one the second time.

- Success is a direction, not a destination.

- Do you expect success or do you just want to avoid failure?

❏ To live, really live, is to succeed.

❏ Declare yourself a success so that you can get on with the rest of your life.

❏ For some people, overnight success takes too long.

❏ One of the biggest stumbling blocks on the road to success is ego.

- Desire and enthusiasm are the fuel of success.

- Sometimes it makes good sense to give yourself an ego enema.

- Success comes in cans. Failure comes in can'ts.

- Success is when where you're going is where you are.

- ❑ Success is when you don't know whether you are working or playing.

- ❑ Genuinely enjoy the success of others. There is enough to go around.

- ❑ Time is money . . . and money is time.

- ❑ Managing your time means taking charge and managing your life.

❑ The two most important words in time management are *no* and *now*.

❑ Many people don't have the time to do something right, but they have the time to do it over.

❑ Time is one of the precious ingredients. Every day brings 86,400 seconds. Whatever isn't used is gone forever.

- ❑ Start sooner and finish faster.

- ❑ Don't waste your time with someone who wastes your time.

- ❑ Put off procrastinating.

- ❑ Time is life. Don't waste it. No one has a lease on life.

❑ Do more by doing less.

❑ Be ruthless with time and gracious with people.

❑ Start your day by doing the worst first. It will make the rest the best.

❑ It is better to be respected and trusted than to be liked.

- Common sense generates uncommon results.

- With professional advisors, it is essential to distinguish between professional and personal opinions.

- Nobody wants what nobody wants.

- All things are difficult before they become easy.

❑ If you try to be all things to all people, you will probably end up being nothing to anyone.

❑ It all depends.

❑ You can't talk your way out of a problem you have behaved your way into.

❑ Retirement has killed more people than old age.

- ❏ It's best not to buy the cheapest parachute, life preserver, fire extinguisher, heart surgery or life insurance.

- ❏ Many millions are mired in mediocrity.

- ❏ The opposite of a great idea is another great idea.

- ❏ Life without risk is not life. It's merely existence.

❏ Jumping to conclusions is not half as good exercise as digging for facts.

❏ Most of what is really important is not taught in school.

❏ Age is a high price to pay for maturity.

❏ We design peace of mind.

- ❑ There is no shortage of success or opportunity.

- ❑ Excellence and quality are their own reward.

- ❑ Who is right is less important than what is right.

- ❑ Decisions are easy when values are clear.

❑ Chemistry and timing are essential to relationships, which are key to success.

❑ For all things there is a first time.

❑ There are two times not to take risk. The first is when you can't afford to, and the second is when you can.

❏ Your life, your career, your character . . . is a movie . . . not a snapshot.

❏ Don't just survive. Thrive and prevail.

❏ Would you really be missing anything if you never watched another show on television?

❏ Good habits separate the best from the rest.

❏ Too much of a good thing is even better.

❏ Try *need reading* rather than *speed reading*. If you don't need to read it, don't.

❏ It's not how you start . . . it's how you finish.

❏ Greatness is that which does not remind you of anything else.

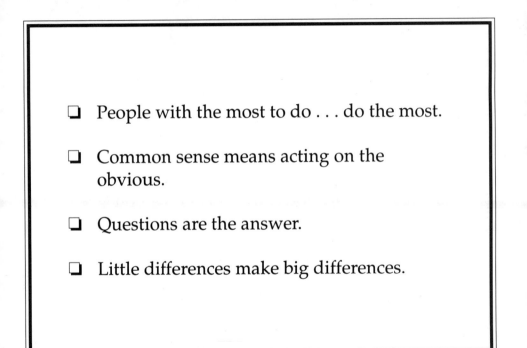

❏ People with the most to do . . . do the most.

❏ Common sense means acting on the obvious.

❏ Questions are the answer.

❏ Little differences make big differences.

❏ The brightest stars emerge from the greatest darkness.

❏ The future's good old days are now.

❏ Every time you make an exception, the exception comes closer to becoming the rule.

❏ You can't see the forest when you're in it.

- ❏ From belief comes conviction and confidence.

- ❏ Hard work generates good luck.

- ❏ If you're going to put all your eggs in one basket, you better pay close attention to the basket.

- ❏ Ideas are the catalysts of change.

❏ There is greatness within each of us.

❏ Why do people always answer questions with another question? Why not?

❏ Common sense is seldom common practice.

❏ Enough is often too much.

- Some people go through life with the accelerator all the way to the floor, but the gear shift is still in neutral.

- Good enough is not good enough.

- If life is a ball, why aren't we dancing?

- The question behind the question is "Why?"

❏ It's smart to pick your friends, but not to pieces.

❏ Eagles don't flock.

❏ Saying "you're right" to someone else doesn't mean you have to be wrong.

❏ Greatness is easier to recognize than to define.

- ❏ You've reached middle age when all you exercise is caution.

- ❏ Short cuts generally aren't.

- ❏ The only thing in life that is guaranteed is death.

- ❏ It is nice to be important, but it is more important to be nice.

❏ The enemies you make by taking a firm stand will have more respect for you than the friends you make by straddling the fence.

❏ Where some fly, others soar.

❏ Taste your words before you say them; you may have to eat them one day.

- ❏ Learn from the mistakes of others - you can never live long enough to make them all yourself.

- ❏ Good company shortens the journey.

- ❏ Group solutions don't solve individual problems.

- ❏ What will be always was.

❑ When someone has taken an unreasonable and inflexible approach to something, it generally means that their position does not coincide with yours, which is both reasonable and flexible.

❑ The most profound insights are just plain common sense, which is uncommon.

❑ Tough times won't last, tough people will.

- ❏ All generalizations should be viewed skeptically, including this one.

- ❏ At the end, all you really own is your integrity.

- ❏ Most parents give their children everything except what they need most . . . limits.

- ❏ Conventional wisdom probably isn't.